199 Treasures of Wisdom on

Talking with God

199 Treasures *of* Wisdom *on* Talking *with* God

Compiled from the writings of
Andrew Murray

BARBOUR
PUBLISHING

Published by Barbour Publishing, Inc., P.O. Box 719, Uhrichsville, Ohio 44683 www.barbourbooks.com

Our mission is to publish and distribute inspirational products offering exceptional value and biblical encouragement to the masses.

ecpa Member of the
Evangelical Christian
Publishers Association

Printed in the United States of America.

*Experience the power of prayer
in your faith walk.*

Andrew Murray (1828–1917) is widely recognized as one of Christendom's foremost authorities on prayer. The South African missionary wrote prolifically on the deeper spiritual life, including *Absolute Surrender*, *The Inner Life*, *The Secret of Adoration*, and *Your Will Be Done*.

Allow Murray's timeless spiritual insights, drawn from his most treasured writings, to penetrate your heart and draw you closer to your heavenly Father with these *199 Treasures of Wisdom on Talking to God*. You'll experience anew the joys and comforts of conversing with your Creator.

1

I must take time to come into God's presence,
to feel my weakness and my need,
and to renew my fellowship with Him.

2

Time alone with the Lord Jesus each day
is the indispensable condition
of growth and power.

3

Even as a father and his child enjoy
being together, so I must have this
intimate fellowship with God each day.

On Talking with God

4

Let this be my chief object in prayer,
to realize the presence of my heavenly Father.
Let my goal be:
"Alone with God."

5

If I seek fellowship with the Father,
I will find Him in His word.

6

May every sight of those in need help urge me
to cry to God who alone can help.

On **Talking** with **God**

7

My source of power in prayer is the Vine.
If I am the branches abiding in Christ,
He will supply the power.

8

Am I spending time in His presence?
Everything depends on this.

9

The greatest happiness of my life is
that I am loved by the Lord Jesus and
can fellowship with Him every day.

O God, you are my God,

earnestly I seek you.

PSALM 63:1

10

O that I would take time daily in
His presence to drink in His love.

11

It is only when I am wholly
surrendered to the Spirit
that I will be able to live
according to God's will.

12

Unless I am on my knees
I cannot live in His love.

13

A life of prayer will make a life of love to Christ,
to other Christians, and to those without Christ.

14

I must ask myself if my prayer is really
in accordance with the will of God
and the Word of God.

15

My hidden prayer life is inseparably
bound up with united prayer.

On Talking with God

16

Time I spend in prayer is
an offering pleasing to God.

17

The real practice of prayer is when
I take hold of God and have communion
and fellowship with Him.

18

To experience real prayer
I must sacrifice my selfish desires.

"Lord, teach us to pray."

LUKE 11:1

19

Isn't it worth the trouble to deny
myself daily in order to meet God?

20

As I pray, my attitude should be
one of silent expectation.

21

When I feel how imperfect my prayer is,
I may bow before God in the confidence that
His Holy Spirit will teach me to pray.

22

I pray for grace to live completely
for God, whether in sharing with
unbelievers or serving His people.

23

I put on Christ by spending
time alone in His presence.

24

When I take the time and the trouble to
spend time with God, my reward will be great.

25

Much time is needed with the Father if
I want to experience the power of God within.

26

In seeking God, in crying for His help—
each time it must be with my whole heart.

27

Spending time with God until I know I desire
to serve Him with my whole heart gives me
the assurance that God hears my prayer.

On **Talking** with **God**

May the words of my mouth
and the meditation of my heart
be pleasing in your sight.

PSALM 19:14

28

Prayer is the one power on earth
that commands the power of heaven.

29

Even in the midst of my daily schedule
I can call out to God.

30

Each day as I spend time in His presence,
let this thought be with me: *Christ is all*.

31

My faith in the great power of
love should prepare me for a life
in communion with God in prayer.

32

As a Christian, I should pray that
I would obey the Word of God
and live in the power of Christ's love.

33

There is only one way that I can love my enemies:
by the love of Christ, sought and found in prayer.

34

If I pray only for myself,
I will not find it easy to be in
the right attitude toward God.

35

Love leads me to prayer.

36

As I wait silently before God,
I become strong in the assurance of faith.

"Therefore I tell you,

whatever you ask for in prayer,

believe that you have received it,

and it will be yours."

MARK 11:24

37

I will take time each day to love God
and believe in Him with a firmer faith.

38

Without love, true holiness is impossible,
so I pray that my love for others will grow.

39

As I walk in fellowship with Him,
I am given strength to be like Him.

40

Loving others may mean tears and heartache,
and much persevering in prayer.

41

I am a channel through which
the highest love can reach its aim.
I will begin to intercede for those around me.

42

If God is waiting to meet me,
it is shortsighted to put other work in His place.

43

If I am to experience God's presence,
I must engage in more definite
and persevering prayer.

44

The scriptural teaching to cry out day
and night in prayer must become my
experience if I am to be an intercessor.

45

Sometimes prayer changes me
more than the circumstances.

"Yet not my will,

but yours be done."

LUKE 22:42

46

Through prayer God can give me strength
for all I do and bring down His power
to work through me in the lives of others.

47

God can bring me the power
to pray that I long for.

48

My relationship with the Father
can become one of continual prayer.

49

As simple as breathing is in the physical life,
so will praying be in my life led by the Spirit.

50

To pray is to enter into God's presence,
commit my need to Him, and leave it there.

51

God wanted people to state what they wanted—
so I should carry my strong desires to Him.

52

When I allow the light of God to illuminate
my life, unbelief will become impossible.

53

The spiritual blessing of God's answer to my
prayer must be accepted in my spirit
before I can see it physically.

54

Prevailing prayer is born
out of my human weakness.

"If you remain in me and
my words remain in you,
ask whatever you wish,
and it will be given you."

JOHN 15:7

55

If I not only seek an answer but
seek after the God who gives the answer,
then I receive the power to know
I have obtained what I have asked.

56

What a privilege it is for me to meet in prayer
with the One who has redeemed me.

57

As I pray, it is the Crucified Christ who comes
to walk with me and in whose power I live.

58

When I meet God in prayer,
His presence is my strength for service.

59

It is only as Jesus Christ dwells in my heart
and life that there can be power in my prayers.

60

As I pray I must be fully convinced of
Christ's words: "I am with you always."

61

If our spiritual life is healthy,
under the power of the Holy Spirit,
praying at all times will be natural.

62

Intercession will become my glory
and my joy when I give myself as
a sacrifice to God for others.

63

The more pointed and definite
my prayer can be, the better.

"But when you pray,
go into your room,
close the door and pray
to your Father,
who is unseen.
Then your Father,
who sees what is done in secret,
will reward you."

MATTHEW 6:6

On Talking with God

64

I expect and look for God's
answers so that I may praise Him.

65

I should pray as a child asks his father,
as simply and trustfully as a child asks for food.

66

It is only as I acknowledge and yield
to the power of the Spirit already in me
that I can pray for His full manifestation.

67

I ought to pray first for all believers
and then for those around me.

68

If I am to pray, I must love.

69

My prayers are not only wishing and asking,
but they must be believing and accepting.

70

My purpose is to pray for believers
and those who do not know God.

71

My prayer and my faith will make a difference.

72

When I am definite in my requests,
it helps me know what answer I am looking for.
I need time with God—to know His presence
and to wait for Him to make Himself known.

The prayer of a righteous man

is powerful and effective.

JAMES 5:16

73

If I seek God with my whole heart,
my whole heart will be in every prayer
with which I come to God.

74

God listens to my every request
with His whole heart.
I will expect the unexpected,
greater than all I ask or think.

75

As I pray, I learn to pray, to believe,
and to expect with increasing boldness.

76

Christ will give me
grace to pray as I should.

77

Prayer is incense that I burn before God.

78

I need to pray in the Spirit if I am to
take hold of God in faith and power.

79

When I seek His nearness, He will give it.
Then it will be easy to pray in faith.

80

I pray, expecting an answer.

81

As I spend time in intercession,
I will see more conversions.

"But I tell you:

Love your enemies and

pray for those who persecute

you, that you may be sons of

your Father in heaven."

MATTHEW 5:44–45

82

As I consciously abide in Him,
I have the liberty to ask what I will in the power
of the new nature, and it will be done.

83

As long as I live and love and hear
and work, I must pray at all times.

84

Through consistent daily prayer,
my whole life becomes devoted to my King
and to the service of His kingdom.

85

I need to experience fellowship
with Christ on His cross if the Spirit
is really to take possession of me.

86

When I pray for the power of the Spirit,
I must yield with my whole heart to His leading.
Lead me to know the indispensable secret
of spiritual health—the prayer life in daily
fellowship with the Father and the Son.

87

What joy it will be to seek God's face
until the earth is full of His glory!

88

I resolve to carry the mark of the
children of God, the great distinction
of the Christian—a life of prayer.

89

Everything in my life is to bear the signature
of Jesus' name. As I learn to live in that name,
I will pray with confidence.

90

I find it a great privilege as I bow in
worship to know that the Father comes
near to me where I am on the earth.

We constantly pray for you,

that our God may count

you worthy of his calling,

and that by his power

he may fulfill every good

purpose of yours and every

act prompted by your faith.

2 THESSALONIANS 1:11

91

When I righteously commit
my whole being to take hold of God,
my prayer is powerful and effective.

92

My prayer receives worth from being
rooted in the sacrifice of Jesus Christ.

93

The most important and profitable time of my
whole day is the time I spend with God.

94

Never let me say:
"I have no time for God."

95

Communion with God through His Word
and prayer is as indispensable to me
as the food I eat and the air I breathe.

96

I need to spend time with God even when
I do not know what to pray.

97

Jesus calls me to separate myself from the world and to yield myself wholeheartedly to praying.

98

Even though I may have to cry day and night to God, I can count on the Father to answer.

99

I ask for the gift of unceasing prayer for the power of God's spirit in all His saints.

I remember you
in my prayers at all times.

ROMANS 1:9–10

100

Once I begin, I will find abundant reason
for persevering in prayer.

101

As a Christian, I should not be afraid
to promise to pray every day.

102

I want to devote my life to the prayer
that can bring down God's blessing.

103

When I draw near to God in humble
prayer, I take the first step in the path
that leads to fellowship with God.

104

I have nothing unless I receive it
from Jesus. Absolute dependence on God
is the secret for power in my work.

105

The spirit of prayer comes when
I turn away from the vanity of time
into the riches of eternity.

106

Self keeps me from prayer, but my heart can be
prepared for prayer by denying the world.

107

To be inspired by God to inward holiness—
I must experience the Spirit of God,
the spirit of love, and the spirit of prayer.

108

The spirit of prayer is stretching with
all my might after the life of God.

On **Talking** with **God**

"This, then,
is how you should pray:
'Our Father in heaven,
hallowed be your name.' "

MATTHEW 6:9

109

Only in humility do I depend on prayer.

110

Self-denial is indispensable if God's redeeming love is to display power and blessing in my life.

111

Nothing can hinder God's holy union with my heart except the decision of my heart to turn away from Him.

112

When earnest prayer has melted away all earthly
passions and desires so that I delight in God
alone, then my prayer changes until I do
not so much pray as I live in God.

113

Prayer is the work of my whole being in absolute
willingness to be what pleases Him.

114

Prayer is an emptying of myself and
my own lusts and desires.

115

Prayer is opening myself for the
light of God to enter me.

116

Turning to God, with or without words,
is the best form of prayer in the world.

117

Prayers not formed according to the real
condition of my heart are like prayers pulled
out of a deep well when I am not in it.

Do not be anxious about
anything, but in everything,
by prayer and petition,
with thanksgiving,
present your requests to God.

PHILIPPIANS 4:6

118

Prayer must come from my heart and
my relationship with God.

119

My times in prayer are meant to
lead me closer to God's heart.

120

Christ will strengthen me for a life of unceasing
prayer as I walk in the light of His countenance.

121

Let me believe God that
He is able to do exceedingly
abundantly above all that I ask or think.

122

My heart will focus on its own state of
prayer as soon as God is its objective.

123

My heart will continually live
and rejoice in God's presence.

124

Every time a truly good desire stirs in my heart,
my heart sends a prayer that reaches God.

～⌾～

125

Through prayer I can have the
Father's presence every moment of the
day for my happiness and strength.

～⌾～

126

I need daily, prayerful fellowship with God if I
am to have His thoughts make their home in me.

"If my people,

who are called by my name,

will humble themselves and

pray and seek my face and

turn from their wicked ways,

then will I hear from heaven

and will forgive their sin

and will heal their land."

2 CHRONICLES 7:14

127

When I bow in deep stillness before God and
believe what He says, then His law will take
possession of my inner life with all its power.

128

Faith for the fulfillment of God's promises can be
found in the discipline of fervent prayer.

129

When I prayerfully turn to God with my whole
heart to plead for what He has promised,
He will fulfill those promises.

On **Talking** with **God**

130

I need to pray that the power of the
Holy Spirit will be deeply felt and that
my faith will be strengthened.

131

As I pray, let me be willing to
accept my place with Him, crucified to
the world, to sin, and to self.

132

In the quietness of prayer let me believe that a
simple and determined surrender of my will to
Him will bring the heart-cleansing I need.

On Talking with God

133

Real prayer is life changing.

134

The closer I draw to God's heartbeat,
the more I realize I need Him.

135

In prayer, I am to be led by the
Spirit every day and every hour.

"And when you stand praying,
if you hold anything
against anyone, forgive him,
so that your Father in heaven
may forgive you your sins."

MARK 11:25

136

Through prayer, God lovingly reveals
areas in our lives that need to change.

137

God will hear my prayer when I hold unflinching
confidence in the power of His promise.

138

My close, abiding fellowship with Christ begins
with deep dependence and unceasing prayer.

139

Faith, led and taught by God's Holy Spirit,
gains the confidence to prayerfully claim:
"I can do all things through Christ
who strengthens me."

140

God asks that I carefully stay in
close fellowship with Him every day in
order that my prayers will be answered.

141

Unbelief dishonors God and
robs me of my heritage.

On Talking with God

142

In silent prayer and adoring faith,
I am assured that God Himself is working
in me all that is well-pleasing in His sight.

143

I have learned how indispensable it is to meet
with God every morning in prayer and allow Him
to take charge of my life for the day.

144

If my conscience is clear, I can come
to God with bold confidence.

"Ask and it will be given to you;

seek and you will find;

knock and the door

will be opened to you.

For everyone who asks receives;

he who seeks finds;

and to him who knocks,

the door will be opened."

MATTHEW 7:7–8

145

Christ will always accept faith that trusts in Him,
even a seed of little faith I plant in my heart.

146

My weak faith in an almighty God can become
the great faith that moves mountains.

147

God wills my holiness. I must not rest
until my will is surrendered
unconditionally to the will of God.

148

In prayer we begin to
realize God's thoughts and will.

149

Every prayer has a value corresponding to
the intention with which I offer it to God.

150

Prayer is a dialogue where I listen
to what the Father says in reply
and then ask for what I need.

151

Prayerful study of the Bible is indispensable
for me to gain power in prayer.

152

Five minutes spent in worship each day will
strengthen my faith for the work of prayer.
God, in His unspeakable love, invites me to come
to Him and communicate freely with Him.

153

The Holy Spirit is purposely given
to intercede for me in prayer.

**Be still before the LORD
and wait patiently for him.**

PSALM 37:7

154

Whenever I come in prayer,
the Lord instructs me to pause long
enough to remember who He is.

155

Let my prayer be something definite, arising
out of the Word I have read and out of the
real soul needs I long to have satisfied.

156

Take time to help a child pray. It will lay a
foundation like none other in their life.

157

Prayer time can become for me a wonder of God's
goodness and a fountain of great joy.

158

I was created in Christ to pray.
It is my nature as a child of God.

159

God's Spirit has been sent into my heart to
draw it up to God in childlike faith.

160

There can be no communion with a
Holy God, no fellowship between heaven
and earth, unless I set apart time for it.

161

God's Word supplies me with material for prayer
and encourages me in expecting His will.

162

It is only in prayer that I can live such a life so
that every word of God be fulfilled in me.

**Come near to God
and he will come near to you.**

JAMES 4:8

163

Though everything may appear cold,
dark, and strained—may I be faithful in
talking with my heavenly Father.

164

To reach the place where the Word
and prayer each have its undivided right over me,
I must be wholly transformed.

165

My day will respond to the morning
watch time spent with God.

166

Prayer opens the way for God to do
His work in and through me.

167

Close and continued fellowship with God
will, in due time, leave its mark on me.

168

When I bow down to pray, the awareness
of my unworthiness will not hinder
me but will help me trust God.

On Talking with God

169

God is always waiting to hear my voice.

170

Only prayer gives my
work its worth and success.

171

What a change it would make
if secret prayer were not only asking for
knowledge or strength, but the giving of my
life into the safekeeping of a faithful God.

On Talking with God

Hear my cry, O God;

listen to my prayer.

From the ends of the earth

I call to you,

I call as my heart grows faint;

lead me to the rock

that is higher than I.

PSALM 61:1–2

On Talking with God

172

I want my spirit to be a listening spirit
waiting to hear what God says.

173

In prayer, I give myself to God; in the
Word, God gives Himself to me.

174

Prayer prepares my heart for receiving the
Word of God from God Himself.

175

The courage to pray for someone is a sign
that you have faith that God is able.

176

My secret communion with God
is the place where I learn the great
lessons concerning God's will.

177

Boldness in prayer comes when I am assured that
the spirit of asking and the thing I've asked for
are both according to the will of God.

178

All the powers of heaven are at my disposal when
I labor in the service of His kingdom.

179

God waits for me to ask for His grace and power.

180

The Holy Spirit knows what the will of God is.
I should learn in faith to pray through the Spirit.

You need to persevere so that

when you have done

the will of God,

you will receive

what he has promised.

HEBREWS 10:36

181

I count it the highest privilege to be a channel
through whose prayers God's blessing can
be brought down to earth.

182

Intercession must not be a passing interest;
it must become an ever-increasing
object of intense desire.

183

In prayer I must expect difficulties which can be
conquered only by determined perseverance.

184

When I know what it is to abide in Christ and to yield to the Holy Spirit, I begin to learn that God will give power in answer to prayer.

185

He who sits upon the throne, and who lives in my heart, has promised that what I ask in His name I will receive.

186

The Holy Spirit breathes God's own desire into me and enables me to intercede for those without Christ.

187

Jesus asks me to yield myself as completely
to God as He did and to pray like He did,
that God's will be done on earth at any cost.

188

Prayer for workers for God's harvest must be
part of my whole life and effort.

189

May I not forget the importance
of praying for our leaders.

When he asks, he must
believe and not doubt,
because he who doubts
is like a wave of the sea,
blown and tossed by the wind.
That man should not think
he will receive anything
from the Lord.

JAMES 1:6–7

190

When I learn to pray not only for my immediate
interests but enlarge my heart to take in the
whole Church and the whole world, my
supplication will have power with God.

191

God will hear me. What a wonderful certainty!
We have God's Word for it.

192

Let me bow in stillness before
God and wait on Him to reveal
Himself as the prayer-hearing God.

193

As little as I comprehend of God,
I can comprehend one of the most wonderful
of His attributes—He hears prayer.
This is a spiritual mystery.

194

If God has blessed my weak prayers,
what will He do if I yield myself
wholly to a life of intercession?

195

I can become God's co-laborer.
My prayer becomes part of God's divine
work of reaching and saving the lost.

196

In the matter of prayer,
God does not demand impossibilities.
He does not ask me to pray without
giving me the grace to do so.

197

There is nothing more worth living for
than this—to satisfy God in His longing
for human fellowship and love.

Ascribe to the LORD
the glory due his name;
worship the LORD in
the splendor of his holiness.

PSALM 29:2

198

May I not rest until I have found a place for the
Mighty One in my heart and have yielded
myself to the work of intercession.

199

May my heart really feel that there is
no honor or joy on earth at all equal
to the unspeakable privilege of waiting
upon God and interceding for
the blessing He delights to give!

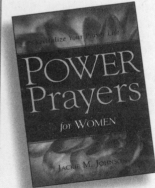